PLUNGE!

LEADER'S GUIDE

PLUNGE!

LEADER'S GUIDE

A Student Edition of *Come Thirsty* by

MAX LUCADO

NELSON REFERENCE & ELECTRONIC
A Division of Thomas Nelson Publishers
Since 1798

www.thomasnelson.com

Compiled by Laura K. Rosser.

Published by Thomas Nelson, Inc., P.O. Box 141000, Nashville, Tennessee, 37214.

Library of Congress Cataloging-in-Publication Data is available.

ISBN 1-4185-0030-5

Printed in the United States of America.

2 3 4 5 — 08 07 06 05 04

PLUN

TABLE OF CONTENTS

"Whoever drinks of
the water that I shall
give him will never
thirst. But the water
that I shall give him
will become in him
a fountain of water
springing up into
everlasting life."

—John 4:14 NKJV

COME THIRSTY READING PLAN

WEEK 1

○ Read the Introduction of *Come Thirsty*. As you read through "Meaghan," her story will sound strangely familiar. As this introduction unfolds, we discover a young woman who is thirsting for something real.

○ Read Chapter 1 of *Come Thirsty*: "The Dehydrated Heart"—Unless we are drinking deeply at the well of God's supply, our hearts become dehydrated—dry, depleted, parched, and weak.

WEEK 2

○ Chapter 2: "Sin Vaccination"—We were all born with a terminal disease— hopelessly infected by sin. See how God made a way for us to live disease free.

○ Chapter 3: "When Grace Goes Deep"—Grace is a gift of God. Take a look at what happens when you try to put conditions on the grace of God. Grace is what defines us.

○ Chapter 4: "When Death Becomes Birth"—Don't allow the dread of death to take away your joy of living.

○ Chapter 5: "With Heart Headed Home"—We live caught between what is and what will be. Our hearts are longing for heaven, and every day that passes brings us closer to home.

WEEK 3

○ Chapter 6: "Hope for Tuckered Town"—Some of us try to live our Christian lives completely in our own power. God offers hope for us when the effort wears us down.

○ Chapter 7: "Waiting for Power"—Before we move forward, sometimes God asks us to wait...and pray.

○ Chapter 8: "God's Body Glove"—The Holy Spirit works with us and through us, hand in glove.

○ Chapter 9: "It's Not Up to You"—God paid too high a price for you to leave you unguarded. The Holy Spirit reminds us of our place in God's heart and comes to our aid in times of weakness.

WEEK 4

WEEK 5

PRAYER OF THE THIRSTY

Lord, I come thirsty. I come to drink,

to receive. I receive Your work

on the cross and in Your resurrection.

My sins are pardoned and my death

is defeated. I receive Your energy.

Empowered by Your Holy Spirit,

I can do all things through Christ

who gives me strength. I receive

Your lordship. I belong to You.

Nothing comes to me that hasn't

passed through You. And I receive

Your love. Nothing can separate

me from Your love. Amen.

INTRODUCTION

Who are we? Busy people. Burdened people. Burned-out people. Strained, stressed, and stretched people, longing for refreshment. These are all symptoms of a dryness deep within. A need. A thirsting. Deprive your soul of spiritual water and it will tell you. Dehydrated hearts send desperate messages. Snarling tempers. Waves of worry. Whispers of guilt and fear. Hopelessness. Sleeplessness. Loneliness. Resentment. Irritability. Insecurity. But God doesn't want us to live like this.

Like the woman at the well, we must recognize our need for living water. Our hearts are parched, dry, dehydrated. We need moisture, a swallow of water, a long, quenching drink. And where do we find water for the soul? "If anyone thirsts, let him come to Me and drink. He who believes in Me, as the Scripture has said, out of his heart will flow rivers of living water" (John 7:37, 38 NKJV). Jesus invites: Are your insides starting to shrivel? Drink me. What H_2O can do for your body, Jesus can do for your heart. Come and see what the Lord can do in your heart! Come ready to receive the refreshment your soul longs for. Come, and come thirsty.

RECEIVE CHRIST'S WORK ON THE CROSS.

RECEIVE THE ENERGY OF HIS SPIRIT.

RECEIVE HIS LORDSHIP OVER YOUR LIFE.

RECEIVE HIS UNENDING, UNFAILING LOVE.

WELL

WEEK 1

Thirsting After Righteousness

"Blessed are those who hunger and thirst for righteousness, for they shall be filled."

—Matthew 5:6 NKJV

FOR THE LEADER

OPENING ACTIVITIES

OPTION 1: AT THE POOL!

You'll Need:

Several weighted diving rings

Scatter the diving rings so that they settle at the bottom of the pool in several different locations. The players will race two at a time to see who can get the most rings, with each person allowed only one time to come up for air. (With very large groups, you may want to race three at a time.) After everyone has participated once, have the winners compete against each other until only the diving champion remains.

Discussion Questions for Afterward:

When the pressure's on, you're totally focused on getting the rings. In your everyday life, do you stay this focused on God, or do you wait 'till the pressure is on?

Because we're humans and have to fill our lungs, coming up for air is what allows us to keep going. What are some ways that we fill our spiritual lungs with air?

How does it feel to dive into the pool with a mission? Are you ready to dive into experiencing God in a deeper way?

OPTION 2: OUTDOORS

You'll Need:

Several large beach towels
Several water balloons

Everyone chooses a partner. Each person grabs the end of a beach towel and balances a water balloon on top of it. Use the towels to throw the balloons up into the air and then to catch them. Whenever a water balloon bursts for a team, that team steps aside. Keep going until even the winning team gets wet!

Discussion Questions for Afterward:

1. Are you feeling spiritually wet these days, or have you gotten too dry? What are some ways you'd like to be refilled?

2. Just as the teams kept tossing the balloons with the towel, we've got to keep active in our spiritual lives. We're on a journey. Spiritually, have you been in the game or on the sidelines?

3. It takes more than one person for this game to work. Likewise, we need other people to share our spiritual journeys. Who are some people you can talk to and

be accountable with over these next few weeks as you experience *Plunge!?*

OPTION 3: INDOORS

You'll Need:
Bibles
A few copies of *Come Thirsty*

Arrange players into two teams determined by whether they like sweet or salty snacks. The sweet team will read the story of the woman at the well in John 4:4–26. The salty team will read the story of Meaghan from *Come Thirsty.* Afterwards, have each team give a brief synopsis of what they read. Then, as a group, compare the two stories.

READING SCRIPTURE ALOUD TOGETHER

○ **John 4:13, 14:** "Jesus answered, 'Everyone who drinks this water will be thirsty again, but whoever drinks the water I give will never be thirsty. The water I give will become a spring of water gushing up inside that person, giving eternal life'" (NCV).

○ **John 7:37, 38:** "On the last and most important day of the feast Jesus stood up and said in a loud voice, 'Let anyone who is thirsty come to me and drink. If anyone believes in me, rivers of living water will flow out from that person's heart, as the Scripture says'" (NCV).

○ **Matthew 5:6:** "Blessed are those who hunger and thirst for righteousness, For they shall be filled" (NKJV).

○ **Matthew 6:33:** "But seek first the kingdom of God and His righteousness, and all these things shall be added to you" (NKJV).

○ **Titus 3:5:** "Not by works of righteousness which we have done, but according to His mercy He saved us" (NKJV).

DISCUSSION QUESTIONS

○ Can you tell when your heart is becoming dehydrated? What are some symptoms of spiritual thirst in your own life? (Answers might include feeling stressed or depressed, being in a bad mood, etc.)

○ Make sure that everyone in your group understands the theme of the *Come Thirsty* Curriculum. Provide the following overview:

During this study, we'll be learning about four ways our thirst can be satisfied: God's work, God's energy, God's lordship, and God's love. They're easy to remember. Just think of the acrostic W-E-L-L.

Receive Christ's **W**ork on the cross.
The **E**nergy of his Spirit.
His **L**ordship over your life.
His unending, unfailing **L**ove.

Drink deeply and often. And out of you will flow rivers of living water.

○ We've grown up hearing such things as "If it sounds too good to be true, it probably is" and "There's no such thing as a free lunch." How do these attitudes affect our understanding of grace? Do you feel as if you should have to *do* something to earn your way into God's favor?

○ Surrounding yourself with worldly things can dull your appetite for what's good and righteous. Have you ever tried to satisfy your spiritual longing with other things? What kinds of substitutes have you tried?

○ We know that our hearts are hungry and thirsty, but how do we cultivate a hunger and thirst for the right things—like righteousness?

OPEN UP THE GROUP TO QUESTIONS

Do you have any questions that came up over the week while you were reading either the book or the daily devotional readings?

INTRODUCTION

Have you ever been in the mood for . . . *something* . . . to eat? You've got the munchies, and you're looking for a snack. The only problem is that you're not quite sure what will satisfy your craving. Something salty? Something sweet? Something chewy? Something crunchy? It's hard to put your finger on what's driving you to rummage through the kitchen. Nothing looks good, so you slam through the cupboards and poke around in the back of the fridge.

Or maybe you're dehydrated . . . aching with thirst. The game is finally over, and you can't wait for a bottle of something cold. Your throat feels so dry that it's distracting you—where is the water cooler? There have to be some soft drinks somewhere!

Our souls are not so different. We get a restless yearning for . . . *something*. Our hearts are hungry. We are driven by a deep thirst. And so we go looking for something—anything—to satisfy our need. If we don't nourish our souls, they grow weak and weary. Deprived of sustenance, we feel depressed, we lose our tempers, we become stressed out. Scripture compares this desperate need with thirst.

Are you thirsty?

1. In the days of Exodus, the children of Israel wandered in the wilderness for forty years. They understood what it meant to be hungry and thirsty. "Hungry and thirsty, their soul fainted in them" (Ps. 107:5 NKJV). How does Isaiah 29:8 describe people's hunger and thirst?

   "When a **hungry** man dreams, and look—he **eats**; but he **awakes**, and his soul is still **empty**; or as when a **thirsty** man dreams, and look—he **drinks**; but he **awakes**, and indeed he is **faint**, and his soul still **craves**" (NKJV)

2. Yet God provided for the physical needs of those who called upon him for relief. The people's dehydrated bodies longed for water, and that is just what God supplied. Match up these promises for refreshment with their texts.

<u>d</u> Nehemiah 9:15   a. God didn't withhold the water from the thirsty.

<u>a</u> Nehemiah 9:20   b. When God led them in deserts, they didn't go thirsty.

<u>f</u> Isaiah 41:17   c. Everyone who thirsts, come to the waters.

<u>b</u> Isaiah 48:21   d. You brought them water out of the rock.

<u>e</u> Isaiah 49:10   e. God has mercy, and leads by springs of water.

<u>c</u> Isaiah 55:1   f. The needy seek water; their tongues fail for thirst.

God supplies our physical needs, sometimes even in miraculous ways. Yet there are times when that doesn't feel like enough. "You have planted much, but you harvest little. You eat, but you do not become full. You drink, but you are still thirsty. You put on clothes, but you are not warm enough. You earn money, but then you lose it all as if you had put it into a purse full of holes" (Hag. 1:6 NCV). We have food to eat and water to drink, but they do not satisfy the longing that pervades our soul. *What am I here for? What is this life about anyway? Why does it feel like I'm missing something?*

We are thirsty, but for what? Where should we go for relief?

> "**You gave them bread from heaven for their hunger, and brought them water out of the rock for their thirst.**"
>
> —Nehemiah 9:15 NKJV

3. Unfortunately, too many people try to quench that inner hunger and thirst with things that can't satisfy. What does Paul say will happen to those who pursue their appetites for earthly things, according to Philippians 3:19?

> If we don't grasp the spiritual nature of our longing, we can too easily be lured aside by earthly things which cannot satisfy our thirst. "Whose end is destruction, whose god is their belly, and whose glory is in their shame—who set their mind on earthly things" (Phil. 3:19 NKJV).

Jesus told his followers, "Blessed are you who hunger now, for you shall be filled" (Luke 6:21 NKJV). That's a wonderful promise! But moments later, he turned this statement upside down. "Woe to you who are full, for you shall hunger" (Luke 6:25 NKJV). Consider this. When people are satisfied with what the world has to offer, they no longer hunger and thirst after spiritual things. They opt for a shortcut. They settle for instant gratification. But those of us who continue to thirst after the living water only Jesus can supply will rely upon him right on into eternity. Our hunger will be satisfied in the very presence of God!

4. King David was a man who understood the longing inside his heart. He knew exactly what he was thirsty for.

○ According to Psalm 42:2, what did David thirst for?

> "I thirst for the living God, when can I go to meet with him?" (Ps. 42:2 NCV).

○ To what did David compare his longing in Psalm 143:6?

> David thirsted for God. "I lift my hands to you in prayer. As a dry land needs rain, I thirst for you" (Ps. 143:6 NCV).

○ What did David do to help fill his longing for God, according to Psalm 63:1?

David compares his longing for God to that of drought-stricken lands, eager and desperate for the rains. "God, you are my God. I search for you. I thirst for you like someone in a dry, empty land where there is no water" (Ps. 63:1 NCV).

5. So what *should* we be hungering for? What *should* we be thirsting after? Jesus tells us in Matthew 5:6.

"Blessed are those who hunger and thirst for righteousness, for they shall be filled" (Matt. 5:6 NKJV).

There's no denying the urgency of our physical thirst. We should heed it. We should drink. But just as we make sure our drinking water is pure, when we seek to quench our thirsty hearts, we must be certain to consume good water. There can be no substitutes.

If you are indeed thirsting after righteousness, then the Lord urges you to drink . . . to drink deeply.

6. Jesus tells us, "Seek first the kingdom of God and His righteousness" (Matt. 6:33 NKJV). So, what is righteousness? Match up these passages, which give us a little overview.

   c Psalm 11:7   a. The heavens declare His righteousness.

   h Psalm 48:10   b. The Sun of Righteousness shall arise.

   a Psalm 50:6   c. The LORD is righteous. He loves righteousness.

   e Psalm 65:5   d. God has given us a robe of righteousness.

_i_ Psalm 119:172   e. God works awesome deeds in righteousness.

_f_ Proverbs 11:19   f. Righteousness leads to life.

_d_ Isaiah 61:10   g. He will be called: THE LORD OUR RIGHTEOUSNESS.

_g_ Jeremiah 23:6   h. God's right hand is full of righteousness.

_b_ Malachi 4:2   i. All of God's commandments are righteousness.

Our first tendency in seeking righteousness is to try to *do* something. The world tells us we have to earn our success. Everywhere we turn, there is pressure to make good grades, to excel in athletics or music, to be the best. But the Lord is not asking us to do anything. We are called upon to receive what he has provided. "Not by works of righteousness which we have done, but according to His mercy He saved us" (Titus 3:5 NKJV).

7. We need to cultivate a hunger and a thirst for righteousness. Yet we cannot achieve a righteous and godly life without God's help!

○ What does God give to us, according to Psalm 24:5?

He shall receive blessing from the LORD, and righteousness from the God of his salvation" (Ps. 24:5 NKJV).

○ God doesn't leave us to fend for ourselves. What does Psalm 23:3 say He will do for us?

"He restores my soul; He leads me in the paths of righteousness for His name's sake" (Ps. 23:3 NKJV).

"Deprive your body of necessary fluid, and your body will tell you. Deprive your soul of spiritual water and your soul will tell you."

—Max Lucado

○ What glorious promise do we find in Psalm 37:6?

> "He shall bring forth your righteousness as
> the light, and your justice as the noonday"
> (Ps. 37:6 NKJV).

8. Throughout the New Testament, we are told that righteousness and right living are only possible by the grace of God. All we need to do is believe. Paul tells us that it is by faith that we are made righteous.

Romans 10:10: "We **believe** with our **hearts**; and so we are **made right** with God; And we use our mouths to say that we **believe**, and so we are saved" (NCV).

2 Corinthians 5:21: "He made Him who **knew** no **sin** to be sin for us, that we might **become** the **righteousness** of God in Him" (NKJV).

Ephesians 4:23, 24: "You were taught to be **made new** in your **hearts**; to become a **new person**. That **new person** is made to be **like God**— made to be truly **good** and **holy**" (NCV).

Philippians 3:9: "Not having my own **righteousness**, which is from the law, but that which is through faith in Christ, the righteousness which is from **God** by **faith**" (NKJV).

> "Blessed
> are those
> who hunger
> and thirst for
> righteousness, for
> they shall be filled."
>
> —Matthew 5:6 NKJV

There is a danger here: sometimes a gift can be given so freely that we take it for granted. We can become numb to our inner thirst for a time. We can sink into laziness or indifference. Scripture uses hunger and thirst to convey a sense of urgency. We are dependent upon God. We cannot live without him. We need him. To keep these important truths before us, we must cultivate our appetite for righteousness. So stir up your hunger. Heed your thirst. Drink, and keep on drinking!

9. Do you hunger and thirst after righteousness? Then the next step is to pursue it!

○ What does Paul urge his son in the faith to pursue in 1 Timothy 6:11?

"Flee these things and pursue righteousness, godliness, faith, love, patience, gentleness" (1 Tim. 6:11 NKJV).

○ What did Jesus do in order to make this pursuit possible, according to 1 Peter 2:24?

Set aside earthly distractions and satisfy your thirst with good things. "Who Himself bore our sins in His own body on the tree, that we, having died to sins, might live for righteousness" (1 Pet. 2:24 NKJV).

○ Where can we turn for help in our pursuit, according to 2 Timothy 3:16?

We could not live for righteousness if Jesus hadn't borne our sins on the cross. "All Scripture is given by inspiration of God, and is profitable for doctrine, for reproof, for correction, for instruction in righteousness" (2 Tim. 3:16 NKJV). God did not leave us wandering and wondering what to do. Everything we need to know for righteous living can be found throughout the pages of His Word.

"He shall bring forth your righteousness as the light, and your justice as the noonday."

—Psalm 37:6 NKJV

10. Jesus is the Source of everything we need. He calls out to everyone, urging them to come.

○ What did Jesus call out to the people in John 7:37?

"Jesus stood and cried out, saying, 'If anyone thirsts, let him come to Me and drink'" (John 7:37 NKJV).

○ According to Revelation 21:6, what does Jesus say that He will freely give?

"I will give of the fountain of the water of life freely to him who thirsts" (Rev. 21:6 NKJV).

○ Who is invited to come and drink, according to Revelation 22:17?

"The Spirit and the bride say, 'Come!' And let him who hears say, 'Come!' And let him who thirsts come. Whoever desires, let him take the water of life freely" (Rev. 22:17 NKJV).

"Now I am right with God, not because I followed the law, but because I believed in Christ. God uses my faith to make me right with him."

—Philippians 3:9 NCV

CONCLUSION

Do you remember the story of the woman at the well? Jesus made an outlandish claim to her: "Whoever drinks of this water will thirst again, but whoever drinks of the water that I shall give him will never thirst. But the water that I shall give him will become in him a fountain of water springing up into everlasting life" (John 4:13,14 NKJV). Like the woman at the well, we recognize our need for living water. We desperately need moisture . . . not just a swallow of water, but a long, quenching drink. Yet where do we find this water for the soul?

Throughout the course of this study, we will be seeking out four ways in which our thirst can be satisfied. God's work. God's energy. His lordship and his love. You'll find them easy to remember. Just think of the word **W-E-L-L**.

Receive Christ's **W**ork on the cross.
The **E**nergy of his Spirit.
His **L**ordship over your life.
His unending, unfailing **L**ove.

Drink deeply and often. And out of you will flow rivers of living water.

PRAYER OF THE THIRSTY

This is the prayer of the thirsty soul who has turned to the only Source of living water. It is the prayer of a heart ready to receive—to drink deeply from the well of God's work, energy, lordship, and love. Take the time each day to pray this prayer aloud. Learn what a vast resource God has made available to you. Make it the cry of your heart.

> *Lord, I come thirsty. I come to drink, to receive. I receive Your work on the cross and in Your resurrection. My sins are pardoned and my death is defeated. I receive Your energy. Empowered by Your Holy Spirit, I can do all things through Christ who gives me strength. I receive Your lordship. I belong to You. Nothing comes to me that hasn't passed through You. And I receive Your love. Nothing can separate me from Your love.*

"In order for Jesus to do what water does, you must let him go where water goes. Deep, deep inside."

—Max Lucado

this week's prayer requests

MEMORY VERSE

"Jesus stood and cried out, saying, 'If anyone thirsts, let him come to Me and drink. He who believes in Me, as the Scripture has said, out of his heart will flow rivers of living water.'"

—John 7:37, 38 NKJV

Suggested Reading for this Week from *Come Thirsty* by Max Lucado:

○ Read the Introduction of *Come Thirsty*: "Meaghan" As you read through "Meaghan," her story will sound strangely familiar. As this introduction unfolds, we discover a young woman who is thirsting for something real.

○ Read Chapter 1 of *Come Thirsty*: "The Dehydrated Heart" Unless we are drinking deeply at the well of God's supply, our hearts become dehydrated—dry, depleted, parched, and weak.

PLUNGE! LEADER'S GUIDE

WELL

RECEIVE CHRIST'S WORK ON THE CROSS.

WEEK 2:

Grace Blockers

"For by grace you have been saved through faith, and that not of yourselves; it is the gift of God."

—Ephesians 2:8 NKJV

FOR THE LEADER

OPENING ACTIVITIES

OPTION 1: AT THE POOL!

You'll Need:
> 2 or 3 inflated plastic balls
> Some sort of prizes (candy bars, soft drinks, toys, etc.) for everyone

Place the prizes at one end of the pool. Tell the swimmers that when they swim across the pool, they'll have a great prize waiting for them. The only catch is, they have to push a ball through the water with them as they swim. Depending on how wide the pool is, have two or three people swim at once.

Discussion Questions for Afterward:

How did it feel to have to push the ball while you were swimming? How much faster could you have swum without it?

Would you have wanted to swim all the way across with the ball if you didn't know you were getting a prize?

Instead of moving freely toward the prize, are there some balls you feel like you're pushing in your spiritual life? Try to identify them.

OPTION 2: OUTDOORS

You'll Need:

Any kind of ball

In the popular cartoon Calvin & Hobbes, sometimes Calvin and Hobbes play Calvinball—a game where they make up the rules as they go along. Divide into teams and make up your own rules for a game of Calvinball. The only rule is that the rules can keep changing!

Discussion Questions for Afterward:

1. Did you like playing Calvinball or did you find it frustrating? Why?

2. Sometimes it feels like there are too many rules to follow—at school, at church, in life. What are some times when you've felt overwhelmed by rules?

3. Are there rules you would get rid of if you could? Which ones?

OPTION 3: INDOORS

You'll Need:

Paper & pencils

Divide into groups of four people. Ask each group, "If you were starting a religion, what would the rules be to join?" Give the groups a few minutes to invent their religions. Then each group will elect a representative to tell the other groups about their religion and its rules. Afterward, discuss which religion was the most popular and why.

READING SCRIPTURE OUT LOUD TOGETHER

○ **1 Peter 1:13:** "So prepare your minds for service and have self-control. All your hope should be for the gift of grace that will be yours when Jesus Christ is shown to you" (NCV).

○ **2 Corinthians 9:8:** "God is able to make all grace abound toward you, that you, always having all sufficiency in all things, may have an abundance for every good work" (NKJV).

○ **Romans 11:6:** "If by grace, then it is no longer of works; otherwise grace is no longer grace. But if it is of works, it is no longer grace; otherwise work is no longer work" (NKJV).

○ **Ephesians 2:7:** "That in the ages to come He might show the exceeding riches of His grace in His kindness toward us in Christ Jesus" (NKJV).

○ **1 Timothy 1:14:** "The grace of our Lord was exceedingly abundant" (NKJV).

DISCUSSION QUESTIONS

○ There are people who block grace by putting limitations and requirements on it. Sometimes this blocking is referred to as legalism. Protecting confidentiality, can you give some examples of legalism from your own life?

○ In the New Testament, the Pharisees are the ultimate legalists. How did their obsession with rules, regulations, and traditions cause trouble between them and Jesus?

○ What is the difference between Christ's work *for* you and Christ's work *in* you?

○ Sometimes we hear inner voices that condemn us— voices that can make us feel guilty, that can mock us, or even accuse us. What do those voices say to you?

○ What's the difference between what those voices tell us about ourselves and what God says about us? Who does God say that you are?

OPEN UP THE GROUP TO QUESTIONS

Do you have any questions that came up during the week while you were reading either the book or the daily devotional readings?

INTRODUCTION

Your heart is thirsty, so you make your way to the water fountain of God's grace for a drink. You've been there before. It's an abundant source of living water. There are crystal clear streams flowing into shining pools at the foot of the throne . . . forever.

Drinking deeply of God's grace is just what your soul needs right now. As you remember how cool and refreshing it is, you break into a run. But as you arrive there, you're astonished to find a handmade sign taped crookedly to the fountain's edge. "No swallowing, please. Taste, but don't drink." That's weird! You look around, wondering if this can be a prank—someone's idea of a joke. Shrugging, you lean your face into the cooling water, but only enough to wet your lips. And so you turn back, with your disappointed heart still longing for refreshment.

Does a sign like that sound absurd? It should. But that's what happens when people try to place limitations on God's grace. They block up the fountain of grace. They monitor our every sip. They stand by with arms folded, directing us to swish and then spit it out, when all the while God intended us to drink . . . to drink deeply.

1. Let's start with grace—unmerited favor. What does the New Testament teach us about God's grace that he extends to us? Match up these truths with the verses where they can be found.

   _k_ 1 Corinthians 15:10   a. Because of grace, we have everlasting hope.

   _e_ Ephesians 1:6   b. By grace we have been made heirs.

   _c_ Colossians 3:16   c. Sing to the Lord with grace in your hearts.

_h_ Colossians 4:6

d. Grace was ours even before time began.

_a_ 2 Thessalonians 2:16

e. By grace, we are accepted in the Beloved.

_d_ 2 Timothy 1:9

f. Be good stewards of God's manifold grace.

_j_ 2 Timothy 2:1

g. We can approach the throne of grace boldly.

_b_ Titus 3:7

h. Let your speech always be with grace.

_g_ Hebrews 4:16

i. Rest your hope fully upon grace.

_i_ 1 Peter 1:13

j. Be strong in grace.

_f_ 1 Peter 4:10

k. By the grace of God, I am what I am.

2. But what good is grace if you don't let it go deep? Look at these verses. More specifically, look at the words used to describe God's grace.

Romans 3:24: "Being justified **freely** by His grace" (NKJV)

Romans 5:20: "Where sin abounded, grace **abounded much more**" (NKJV)

2 Corinthians 9:8: "God is able to make all grace **abound** toward you, that you, always having all sufficiency in all things, may have an **abundance** for **every** good work" (NKJV)

Ephesians 2:7: "That in the ages to come He might show the **exceeding** riches of His grace in His kindness toward us in Christ Jesus" (NKJV)

1 Timothy 1:14: "The grace of our Lord was **exceedingly abundant**" (NKJV)

Abundant. Free. Sufficient. Rich. God's grace is excessive—infinitely bigger than our need. In fact, it's *all* we need. But there were people in the early church who tried to block the flow of grace. They wanted to set limits on it. They tried to control it. They molded it to fit into their traditions. They redefined it to suit their purposes. And they deceived God's people by claiming that what they said was true.

3. What new rules did some people try to impose on Gentile believers, according to Acts 15:1?

   "Then some people came to Antioch from Judea and began teaching the non-Jewish believers: 'You cannot be saved if you are not circumcised as Moses taught us'" (Acts 15:1 NCV). How outrageous! There is no commandment of God that says, "Thou shalt be circumcised, or thou canst not become a Christian." They tried to adapt grace to fit into their traditions, and received an apostolic rebuke for it.

> "God refuses to compromise the spiritual purity of heaven. Herein lies the awful fruit of sin. Lead a godless life and expect a godless eternity. Spend a life telling God to leave you alone and He will."
>
> —**Max Lucado**

4. The Galatian church also ran into problems. Paul was astonished by how far off track they had been lured!

Galatians 1:6, 7: "God, by his grace through Christ, called you to become his people. So I am **amazed** that you are **turning away** so quickly and believing something **different** than the **Good News.** Really, there is **no other** Good News. But some people are confusing you; they want to **change** the Good News of Christ" (NCV)

Legalism. Grace blockage. It's thinking that your heavenly Father might let you in the gate, but you've got to earn your place at the table. God hands you the study guide, but you've still got to pass the test. Heaven gives you the boat, but you've got to row it yourself if you ever want to see the other shore. These lies don't allow you to receive God's work. They try to tell you to earn it.

5. Yet grace, by its very definition, means we can't earn it. Why does Paul say in Romans 11:6 that grace cannot come by works?

> "If by grace, then it is no longer of works; otherwise grace is no longer grace. But if it is of works, it is no longer grace; otherwise work is no longer work" (Rom. 11:6 NKJV).

Grace by faith is a theme Paul teaches over and over again. "People cannot do any work that will make them right with God. So they must trust in him, who makes even evil people right in his sight. Then God accepts their faith and that makes them right with him" (Rom. 4:5 NCV). There's one way, and only one. By grace, through faith.

> If grace had to be earned, it couldn't be called grace. As another translation puts it, "If they could be made God's people by what they did, God's gift of grace would not really be a gift" (NCV).

6. Why does Ephesians 2:8, 9 say we have no reason to boast over our place in God's family?

> "For by grace you have been saved through faith, and that not of yourselves; it is the gift of God, not of works, lest anyone should boast" (Eph. 2:8, 9 NKJV). How can you boast about something you did not do? God did all the work. All we did was receive the gift.

When faith changes from grace-receiving to law-keeping, beware! Be careful when salvation is limited to people who can meet the standards and make the grade. The truth is that we can't earn God's grace. We can only receive God's work. And that's when our hearts are able to drink deeply from the well of living water.

7. What's this work that we must receive? Christ's work on the cross. The Bible puts the question another way: "What must I do to be saved?" (Acts 16:30 NKJV).

○ How is this question answered in Acts 16:31?

> "Believe in the Lord Jesus and you will be saved" (Acts 16:31 NCV).

○ According to 2 Corinthians 5:21, how were we freed from sin?

> "Christ had no sin, but God made him become sin so that in Christ we could become right with God" (2 Cor. 5:21 NCV).

○ What did Jesus say we have to believe in order to be saved, according to John 8:24?

> "I told you that you would die in your sins. Yes, you will die in your sins if you don't believe that I am he" (John 8:24 NCV). Salvation hinges on Jesus Christ and our belief. Do you believe he is who he said he is? Have you received God's grace by faith?

> **"Sin may, and will, touch you, discourage you, distract you, but it cannot condemn you."**
>
> **—Max Lucado**

And so our sins are forgiven. Christ responded to universal sin with a universal sacrifice. He took on the sins of the entire world—this is Christ's work *for* you. But the salvation we receive doesn't stop there. Jesus not only took your place on the cross—he takes his place in your heart. This is Christ's work *in* you.

8. How does Paul describe people who have drunk deeply from God's water fountain of grace?

○ What does Romans 4:7 say about those who have received Christ's work *for* them?

"Happy are they whose sins are forgiven, whose wrongs are pardoned" (Rom. 4:7 NCV).

○ How have our lives been changed by Christ's work *in* us, according to Romans 6:6?

The New King James Version reads, "Blessed are those whose lawless deeds are forgiven, and whose sins are covered." (Rom. 4:7 NKJV) That is Christ's work *for* us. And what about His work *in* us? "We know that our old life died with Christ on the cross so that our sinful selves would have no power over us and we would not be slaves to sin" (Rom. 6:6 NCV).

You're still going to occasionally sin. When you do, remember: sin may touch you, but it can't claim you—because Christ is in you! Trust his work *for* you. He took your place on the cross. And trust his work *in* you. Your heart is his home, and his home is completely sin-free.

9. There are many voices, telling you who you should be and what you should do. Which ones have you heard lately? Which ones have you been listening to?

Other people are very willing to let you know what they think of you and of your choices. They point out your flaws. They dig up past mistakes. They tell you what they would do in your place. But they cannot define you. Grace defines you. Only God can tell you who you are. His is the only opinion that matters.

❑ You don't fit in.

❑ You don't measure up.

❑ You ought to know better.

❑ You've made too many mistakes.

❑ You've got to try harder.

❑ You're doing it all wrong.

❑ You're not making a difference.

❑ You're not popular/talented/smart/athletic/good/
_____ enough.

❑ Face it, you're a failure.

❑ Nobody really cares about you.

❑ You can't do that.

❑ It's your own fault.

❑ You're too short/tall/big/small/wide/thin/_____.

❑ You'll never amount to anything.

❑ I told you so.

Remember—these voices don't define you! You are who *God* says you are! Grace defines you. People may have opinions, but they hold no weight. Only God does. His is the only opinion that matters—and according to him, you are his. Period.

10. Who does God say you are? What does Ephesians 2:10 tell us?

"God has made us what we are. In Christ Jesus, God made us to do good works, which God planned in advance for us to live our lives doing" (Eph. 2:10 NCV). We are who God made us to be. Unique. Special. Gifted for a purpose. Planned on. In other translations, we are God's "workmanship," his "handiwork," his "masterpiece."

CONCLUSION

Receive God's work. Drink deeply from his well of grace. Your deeds don't save you. And your deeds don't keep you saved. God does. Don't just read this truth—trust and believe it! Let this be your constant prayer: "Lord, I receive Your work. My sins are forgiven." Trust the work of God *for* you. Then trust the presence of Christ *in* you. Take frequent, refreshing drinks from his water fountain of grace. You need regular reminders that you are not damaged goods! Don't live like you are.

PRAYER OF THE THIRSTY

Return to this prayer, paying close attention to the heartfelt meaning in the first few sentences. You came to God thirsty, and now he is answering you with the satisfying work of grace. Savor Christ's work for you and in you. Enjoy it. Let the truth of salvation fill you up, quench your thirst, and refresh your soul.

> *Lord, I come thirsty. I come to drink, to receive. I receive Your work on the cross and in Your resurrection. My sins are pardoned and my death is defeated. I receive Your energy. Empowered by Your Holy Spirit, I can do all things through Christ who gives me strength. I receive Your lordship. I belong to You. Nothing comes to me that hasn't passed through You. And I receive Your love. Nothing can separate me from Your love. Amen.*

this week's prayer requests

MEMORY VERSE

"For by grace you have been saved through faith, and that not of yourselves; it is the gift of God, not of works, lest anyone should boast. For we are His workmanship, created in Christ Jesus for good works, which God prepared beforehand that we should walk in them"

—Ephesians 2:8–10 NKJV

Suggested Reading for this Week from *Come Thirsty* by Max Lucado:

○ Chapter 2: "Sin Vaccination" We were all born with a terminal disease—hopelessly infected by sin. See how God made a way for us to live disease-free.

○ Chapter 3: "When Grace Goes Deep" Grace is a gift of God. Take a look at what happens when you try to put conditions on the grace of God. Grace is what defines us.

○ Chapter 4: "When Death Becomes Birth" Don't allow the dread of death to take away your joy of living.

○ Chapter 5: "With Heart Headed Home" We live, caught between what is and what will be. Our hearts are longing for heaven, and every day that passes brings us closer to home.

PLUNGE! LEADER'S GUIDE

WELL

**RECEIVE THE ENERGY
OF HIS SPIRIT.**

WEEK 3

Redefining Prayer

*"'Not by might nor by power, but by My Spirit,' says the L*ORD* of hosts."*

—Zechariah 4:6 NKJV

OPENING ACTIVITIES

OPTION 1: AT THE POOL!

Lead the group in playing "Marco Polo." Choose someone to be "It." The leader (It) must keep eyes closed while trying to find and tag someone else. The others can swim wherever they want, but they must stay in the pool. Whenever the "It" person calls out "Marco!", everyone else must answer, "Polo!" Once the "It" person is able to tag someone else, that person becomes the new "It."

Discussion Questions for Afterward:

How did you feel when you were "It"? Was it hard to catch somebody else? Have you ever felt like you were calling out to God, but you couldn't tell where He was?

Instead of being able to use your eyes, in this game you have to listen. When you pray to God, are you the one doing all the talking—or do you wait to listen?

Sometimes it feels like you're going to be "It" forever, chasing after everyone else. Have you ever chased after God this way? What were the results?

OPTION 2: OUTDOORS

You'll Need:

Several water balloons
Stopwatch
Kids who don't mind getting wet!

Have everyone get in a circle. Instruct one person to toss a water balloon to another person. Before passing it on, each person has ten seconds to call out a typical (but clean) phrase/slang word (e.g., "dude"), or they move "out" of the circle. (For larger groups, when a water balloon bursts, that person is also "out.") The first person has ten seconds to say any slang/phrase word (e.g. "dis," "drat"), then the next person has ten seconds to say what the slang/phrase word means. Continue until there are only two people left. Whoever doesn't get stumped—or wet—wins!

Discussion Questions for Afterward:

Do you use a lot of slang? However you talk, God understands you, and he listens Jesus taught us to pray using ordinary, honest words.

Did you know the meaning of most of the slang words presented during the game? Why or why not? Whether it's our first words as a baby or the slang we pick up at school, we tend to learn by hearing other people say things.

Do we have "Christian slang"—words that we toss around as Christians, that people outside the church might not know? Can you give some examples? How do you think people feel when they don't know "our" slang?

OPTION 3: INDOORS

Divide into two teams. The first person in Team A chooses a familiar kids' song ("Mary Had a Little Lamb," "Twinkle Twinkle Little Star," "Yankee Doodle," "Row Row Row Your Boat," etc.). The first person in Team B makes up a slang word for one of the lyrics in the song. The next person in Team A has to sing the song with the new lyrics and then choose a new slang word to add. Play continues to alternate between the teams as each person sings the song with increasing slang. Anyone using the normal lyrics is out of the game! Afterward, talk about how hard it can be sometimes to remember all the right words—and how this isn't what God wants or expects from us in prayer.

> "Pray in the Spirit at all times with all kinds of prayers, asking for everything you need. To do this you must always be ready and never give up."
>
> —Ephesians 6:18 NCV

READING SCRIPTURE OUT LOUD TOGETHER

O **Ephesians 6:18:** "Pray in the Spirit at all times with all kinds of prayers, asking for everything you need. To do this you must always be ready and never give up" (NCV).

O **Jeremiah 29:12:** "You will call upon Me, and go and pray to Me, and I will listen to you" (NKJV).

○ **Romans 8:26:** "The Spirit also helps in our weaknesses. For we do not know what we should pray for as we ought, but the Spirit Himself makes intercession for us with groanings which cannot be uttered" (NKJV).

○ **Psalm 27:8:** "When You said, 'Seek My face,' My heart said to You, 'Your face, LORD, I will seek'" (NKJV).

○ **Zechariah 4:6:** "'Not by might nor by power, but by My Spirit,' says the LORD of hosts" (NKJV).

DISCUSSION QUESTIONS

○ Review last week's lesson. Also, remind everyone that to quench our spiritual thirst, we go to the W-E-L-L:

During this study, we'll be learning about four ways our thirst can be satisfied: God's work, God's energy, God's lordship, and God's love. They're easy to remember. Just think of the acrostic W-E-L-L.

Receive Christ's **W**ork on the cross.
The **E**nergy of his Spirit.
His **L**ordship over your life.
His unending, unfailing **L**ove.

Drink deeply and often. And out of you will flow rivers of living water.

○ Would you say that your Christian walk has a lot of energy? If not, how would you describe it?

○ What kind of power is available to believers—*all* believers?

○ Max Lucado says, "Change your definition of prayer. Think of prayers as less an activity *for* God and more an awareness *of* God." How does this statement affect your prayers in a practical way? What things change?

○ Ask some of the questions from the conclusion of Lesson 3:

What would life be like if you never learned about the energy that's available through the Holy Spirit? Would you feel like your spiritual walk was all up to you? Would you have to rely on your own strength, smarts, and willpower to please God? All the responsibility for your spiritual state would rest on your own shoulders. Trying to stay righteous and close to God would stress you out. You'd be exhausted! What kind of life would you lead?

OPEN UP THE GROUP TO QUESTIONS

Do you have any questions that came up during the week while you were reading either the book or the daily devotional readings?

INTRODUCTION

We don't like being tired. We were made to flourish and thrive—to have energy. But when you don't drink from the well of God's provision, you become spiritually thirsty. You dry out. Instead of standing strong, you give into weakness. You lose your passion for living. The littlest thing can start stressing you out. You thought you had it down, but now it's coming apart.

We don't like being tired, but for some reason we stay this way. Why? Because we don't ask for the energy we need. God's energy. Pulsing power. Supernatural strength. Spiritual biceps. Well, how do we ask the Father for this kind of strength?

We pray.

"The Spirit helps us with our weakness. We do not know how to pray as we should. But the Spirit himself speaks to God for us, even begs God for us with deep feelings that words cannot explain."

—Romans 8:26 NCV

1. Jesus promised his disciples that he would provide them with the power they needed.

Luke 24:49: "Behold I send the **Promise** of My Father upon you; but tarry in the city of Jerusalem until you are **endued** with **power** from **on high**" (NKJV).

"You shall **receive power** when the **Holy Spirit** has **come upon** you" (Acts 1:8 NKJV).

When does power come? Thankfully, it's not up to us to generate this kind of energy. It is a gift from God—all we have to do is receive it. Power comes as we allow the God who saved us to change us. Power comes as we allow his Spirit to work in us. Power comes when we get rid of deep-rooted sin through confession. Power comes when we go through the day seeking God's Spirit. And power comes when we pray.

2. Prayer is a powerful thing! What does Paul urge every believer to do in these verses?

○ Romans 12:12

Pray! "Pray at all times" (Rom. 12:12 NCV).

○ Ephesians 6:18

"Pray in the Spirit at all times with all kinds of prayers, asking for everything you need. To do this you must always be ready and never give up (Eph. 6:18 NCV).

○ 1 Thessalonians 5:17

"Pray continually" (1 Thess. 5:17 NCV).

3. Listen to how King David pleads with God to hear him: "Hear me when I call, O God of my righteousness! . . . Have mercy on me, and hear my prayer" (Ps. 4:1 NKJV). We can learn two lessons from David: we need to pray continually, and we need to pray with confidence.

> "God never promises an absence of distress. But he does promise the assuring presence of his Holy Spirit."
>
> —Max Lucado

○ According to Jeremiah 29:12, what does God do?

"You will call upon Me, and go and pray to Me, and I will listen to you" (Jer. 29:12 NKJV).

○ God not only hears our prayers, but he also responds. When does Isaiah 65:24 say God answered the call of his people?

"It shall come to pass that before they call, I will answer; and while they are still speaking, I will hear" (Is. 65:24 NKJV).

○ Because of Jesus' sacrifice, we can approach God with confidence. What does Hebrews 4:16 tell us to do to find the help we need?

<u>"Let us therefore come boldly to the throne of grace, that we may obtain mercy and find grace to help in time of need" (Heb. 4:16 NKJV).</u>

None of us pray as much as we should . . . but all of us pray more than we think. In those times when we gasp and sigh and moan. When tears slide silently down our cheeks. When our whole heart aches with need. When we hurt so much we have no words. Those are the times when the Spirit comes alongside and helps us in our weakness.

4. Just how does the Spirit help us, according to Romans 8:26?

<u>"The Spirit also helps in our weaknesses. For we do not know what we should pray for as we ought, but the Spirit Himself makes intercession for us with groanings which cannot be uttered" (Rom. 8:26 NKJV). The Spirit prays with us and for us. He makes sure you get heard.</u>

Many people talk about prayer as a spiritual discipline. We read about saints who dedicated hours and hours to intercession, and we feel guilty because we don't measure up. A lot of us want to spend more time in prayer. But who has time to sit quietly, with their hands folded and their eyes shut? Try this: change your definition of prayer. Think of prayer as less of an *activity* for God, and more of an *awareness* of God. Seek to live so that every moment, every day, you're aware of him. Acknowledge his presence everywhere you go.

5. God promises that he is present with everyone who belongs to him. Some people race through life at a hundred miles a minute, never seeing or acknowledging God's hand. But those who are aware of God's presence have some powerful responses.

f Exodus 33:14   a. In God's presence is fullness of joy.

a Psalm 16:11   b. The righteous will dwell in God's presence.

d Psalm 21:6   c. Come into God's presence with singing.

g Psalm 68:8   d. In God's presence are gladness and blessing.

c Psalm 100:2   e. In God's presence are times of refreshment.

b Psalm 140:13   f. In God's presence is rest.

e Acts 3:19   g. In God's presence the earth itself shakes.

6. David assures us, "The LORD is close to everyone who prays to him, to all who truly pray to him" (Ps. 145:18 NCV).

○ What encouragement and promise was offered to Joshua in Joshua 1:9?

"Remember that I commanded you to be strong and brave. Don't be afraid, because the LORD your God will be with you everywhere you go" (Josh. 1:9 NCV).

> "All believers have God in their hearts. But not all believers have given their whole heart to God."
>
> —Max Lucado

❍ What promise did Jesus make to his followers in Matthew 28:20?

<u>"I will be with you always, even until the end of this</u>
<u>age" (Matt. 28:20 NCV).</u>

❍ What dwells in us, according to John 14:17?

<u>"The Spirit of truth . . . you know Him, for He dwells</u>
<u>with you and will be in you" (John 14:17 NKJV).</u>

❍ What does Deuteronomy 30:14 say we should keep near to us?

<u>"No, the word is very near you. It is in your mouth and</u>
<u>in your heart so you may obey it" (Deut. 30:14 NCV).</u>

Often we have to wait a while for the power we've prayed for. This doesn't mean doing nothing or staying busy so we'll forget about it. We're still seeking. We're listening attentively for an answer. Waiting means watching. If you're waiting on a bus, you're watching for the bus. If you're waiting on God, you're watching for God—searching for God—hoping for God.

7. Knowing that God is present with us is a good thing. But it's infinitely better to seek *God* out. Go after him. Look for his hand. Search for him. Chase after him.

<u>f</u> Ezra 7:10   a. Those who seek the LORD will praise Him.

<u>d</u> Psalm 9:10   b. Those who seek Him will lack for nothing.

<u>a</u> Psalm 22:26   c. Seek the LORD's face evermore.

<u>h</u> Psalm 27:4   d. The LORD does not forsake those who seek Him.

<u>b</u> Psalm 34:10   e. Those who seek the LORD will rejoice.

_e_ Psalm 105:3   f. Your heart must be prepared to seek.

_c_ Psalm 105:4   g. Seek the LORD, seek righteousness, seek humility.

_i_ Isaiah 55:6   h. Seek the chance to see the beauty of the LORD.

_g_ Zephaniah 2:3   i. Seek the LORD while He may be found.

8. Guess what? God is ready to be found by those who seek him!

○ What does David say that God is watching for in Psalm 14:2?

   "The LORD looks down from heaven upon the children of men, to see if there are any who understand, who seek God" (Ps. 14:2 NKJV).

○ What does God ask us to do, and what should our response be, according to Psalm 27:8?

   God is watching for seekers, and he welcomes their pursuit. "When You said, 'Seek My face,' My heart said to You, 'Your face, LORD, I will seek'" (Ps. 27:8 NKJV).

"You can look for the LORD your God, and you will find him if you look for him with your whole being."

—Deuteronomy 4:29 NCV

○ This is no casual game of hide-and-seek. How does Deuteronomy 4:29 say we should seek after God?

   God wants us searching for him, watching for him, following after him. "You will seek the LORD your God, and you will find him if you seek him with all your heart and with all your soul" (Deut. 4:29 NKJV). Seek and you shall find, so long as you throw yourself wholeheartedly into the search. God wants us all, heart, mind, and body.

The Spirit fills us as prayers flow through us. Do you want to be filled with strength? Well, of course! Then pray, "Lord, I receive Your energy. Empowered by Your Holy Spirit, I can do all things through Christ who gives me strength."

9. It's not up to us. We can't depend on ourselves, because we're human. We have limits. True strength comes from God. So pray for his energy, for his power, for his Spirit.

"'Not by **might** (no amount of guts, stamina, or determination will help), nor by **power** (don't rely on independence, authority, or willpower), but by **My Spirit** (spiritual strength is the power we need),' says the Lord of hosts" (Zech. 4:6 NKJV).

10. When our hearts thirst for energy, all we have to do is turn to the Source of living water for the strength we need. "But You, O Lord, do not be far from Me; O My Strength, hasten to help Me!" (Ps. 22:19 NKJV).

Exodus 15:2: "The Lord is my **strength and song**."

2 Samuel 22:33: "God is my **strength and power**."

Psalm 73:26: "God is the **strength of my heart and my portion forever**."

Psalm 20:6: "He will answer . . . with **the saving strength of His right hand**."

CONCLUSION

What would life be like if you never learned about the energy that's available through the Holy Spirit? Would you feel like your spiritual walk was all up to you? Would you have to rely on your own strength, smarts, and willpower to please God? All the responsibility for your spiritual state would rest on your own shoulders. Trying to stay righteous and close to God would stress you out. You'd be exhausted! What kind of life would you lead? A dry, dead, and prayerless one.

But what happens to the soul who seeks God? What happens to the woman who taps into God's vast resources? What happens to the man who believes in the work of the Spirit? Who really believes? Is there a difference? Yes . . . definitely! Your shoulders lift as you quit trying to save yourself. Your knees bend as they discover the power of the praying Spirit. And best of all, you have a quiet confidence that comes from knowing it's not up to you.

PRAYER OF THE THIRSTY

Lift up this prayer once again to the Lord. You've learned what it means to receive his work. Now you're reaching out to him, asking to receive his energy. Repeat this prayer again and again through the week ahead. Remember where your strength comes from . . . and learn to rely on it.

> *Lord, I come thirsty. I come to drink, to receive. I receive Your work on the cross and in Your resurrection. My sins are pardoned and my death is defeated. I receive Your energy. Empowered by Your Holy Spirit, I can do all things through Christ who gives me strength. I receive Your lordship. I belong to You. Nothing comes to me that hasn't passed through You. And I receive Your love. Nothing can separate me from Your love.*

this week's prayer requests

MEMORY VERSE

*"Let us therefore come boldly
to the throne of grace, that
we may obtain mercy and find
grace to help in time of need."*

—Hebrews 4:16 NKJV

Suggested Reading for this Week from
Come Thirsty by Max Lucado:

○ Chapter 6: "Hope for Tuckered Town" Some of us try
to live our Christian lives completely in our own power.
God offers hope for us when the effort wears us down.

○ Chapter 7: "Waiting for Power" Before we move
forward, sometimes God asks us to wait . . . and pray.

○ Chapter 8: "God's Body Glove" The Holy Spirit works
with us and through us, hand in glove.

○ Chapter 9: "It's Not Up to You" God paid too high a
price for you to leave you unguarded. The Holy Spirit
reminds us of our place in God's heart and comes to
our aid in times of weakness.

notes

PLUNGE! LEADER'S GUIDE

W-E-L-L

RECEIVE HIS LORDSHIP OVER YOUR LIFE.

WEEK 4

Choosing Peace

"You cannot add any time to your life by worrying about it."

—Matthew 6:27 NCV

OPENING ACTIVITIES

OPTION 1: AT THE POOL!

Lead the group in playing Sharks & Minnows—basically a pool version of Tag. Choose one person to be the shark; everyone else is a minnow. The minnows swim around trying to escape the shark. When the shark tags someone, he or she becomes a shark, too. The last minnow is the winner!

Discussion Questions for Afterward:

1. In your life, do you feel more like a shark or a minnow? Why?

2. When you're a minnow, you're always swimming around trying to escape the shark. What keeps you running around in your day-to-day life?

3. What are some "sharks" that you find yourself worrying about?

OPTION 2: OUTDOORS

You'll Need:

> An area with lots of hiding places

Play silent hide-and-seek. Select one person to be "It" and have him or her choose a secret word. While the "It" person counts to fifty, everyone else goes and hides. All players can move around as much as they want to, but no one is allowed to talk or make any noise. When "It" finds and tags another player, s/he whispers the secret word to that player, who also becomes "It." Play continues until everyone knows the secret word. The last one caught wins!

Discussion Questions for Afterward:

> Did you stay in one place or did you do a lot of running around? Why? How does your answer relate to how you live your life?

> Which do you like best—hiding or seeking? Which do you find yourself doing more of spiritually?

> Sometimes God does things that get our attention loud and clear. Other times he whispers words to us softly. Has God ever whispered a word of peace to you?

OPTION 3: INDOORS

You'll Need:

> 2 large sheets of poster board, easel paper, or dry erase boards
> Markers for writing

Have the girls go to one side of the room and the guys to the other. Each group will make a giant "worry list" of anything and everything that they worry about. Afterward, come back together and choose someone from each group to go over his/her worry list. You'll probably find that there are more similarities than differences!

READING SCRIPTURE OUT LOUD TOGETHER

○ **Psalm 37:8:** "Do not fret—it only causes harm" (NKJV).

○ **Matthew 6:34:** "Do not worry about tomorrow" (NKJV).

○_**Psalm 115:3:** "Our God is in heaven. He does what he pleases" (NCV).

○ **Isaiah 46:10:** "When I plan something, it happens. What I want to do, I will do" (NCV).

○ **Philippians 4:7:** "The peace of God, which surpasses all understanding, will guard your hearts and minds through Christ Jesus" (NKJV).

○ **Colossians 3:15:** "Let the peace of God rule in your hearts, to which also you were called in one body; and be thankful" (NKJV).

○ **1 Peter 5:7:** "Casting all your care upon Him, for He cares for you" (NKJV).

○ **Ephesians 1:11:** "In Christ we were chosen to be God's people, because from the very beginning God had decided this in keeping with his plan. And he is the One who makes everything agree with what he decides and wants" (NCV).

DISCUSSION QUESTIONS

○ *Come Thirsty* urges us to return to the W-E-L-L. Take a few minutes to review the outline of the lesson plans with your group.

During this study, we'll be learning about four ways our thirst can be satisfied: God's work, God's energy, God's lordship, and God's love. They're easy to remember. Just think of the acrostic W-E-L-L.

Receive Christ's **W**ork on the cross.
　　The **E**nergy of his Spirit.
　　　　His **L**ordship over your life.
　　　　　　His unending, unfailing **L**ove.

Drink deeply and often. And out of you will flow rivers of living water.

○ What does it mean to say that worry is irrelevant (pointless)? What does it mean to say that worry is irreverent (not trusting God)?

○ Psalm 37:8 says, "Do not fret—it only causes harm." What kind of harm does worry cause?

○ When it comes to the character of God, you may have heard of the three O's—omnipresent, omniscient, omnipotent. When we say God is omnipotent—all-powerful—do we really believe that he can do anything? When we say God is omniscient—all-seeing/knowing—do we believe that he is sovereign? What do these facts mean in our everyday lives? What are some practical results of these truths?

○ What does lordship mean? How can God's lordship be a source of strength for our hearts and help quench our spiritual thirst?

○ If worry is like a deadly plague, prayer and thanksgiving are the antidotes. How do prayer and thanksgiving counteract the plague of worry?

○ What does it mean to say, "Peace rules in our hearts"? How is this peace able to then guard our hearts?

OPEN UP THE GROUP TO QUESTIONS

Do you have any questions that came up during the week while you were reading either the book or the daily devotional readings?

INTRODUCTION

What's there to worry about? Plenty. We worry about big stuff and little stuff, things we did and things we're going to do, things we're responsible for and things we have no control over. We worry about teachers and tests, decisions and deadlines, risks and relationships. About our looks, about our grades, about what people think of us.

Wouldn't you love to stop worrying? Could you use a strong shelter from life's harsh elements? A stress-free zone to let your hair down and just chill for a while? God offers you just that! In fact, he offers you something even better—the possibility of a worry-free life. Not just less worry, but no worries at all!

You might be thinking, "Are you kidding?" Worry can be hard to shake. It comes so naturally to most of us. But Jesus wasn't kidding when he told us not to worry in this world. In fact, there are two words that summarize his opinion of worry: irrelevant (pointless) and irreverent (not trusting God).

1. We worry every day about everyday things. Jesus knew this, so when he was on earth, he talked a lot about our worries. We can read about it in the gospels. What do each of these verses say we tend to worry over?

○ Psalm 37:1

   <u>Do not worry about evildoers (Ps. 37:1).</u>

○ Psalm 37:7

   <u>Do not worry when men plan wicked schemes (Ps. 37:7).</u>

○ Matthew 6:25

   <u>Do not worry about your life (Matt. 6:25).</u>

○ Matthew 6:28

Do not worry about what you will wear (Matt. 6:28).

○ Matthew 6:31

Do not worry about what you will eat or drink (Matt. 6:31).

○ Matthew 6:34

Do not worry about tomorrow (Matt. 6:34).

2. David advises, "Do not fret—it only causes harm" (Ps. 37:8 NKJV). What's the point of worrying, according to Jesus in Matthew 6:27?

"You cannot add any time to your life by worrying about it" (Matt. 6:27 NCV). Jesus dismisses worry as useless. Worry can't change things.

Worry means our faith is fragile. In essence we're saying we doubt God's ability to take care of us. We aren't so sure he knows what he's doing. We're not convinced that he really has our best interests in mind. And so we're reluctant to give over control—to accept God's lordship over our lives. It's subtle. It's even unintentional—we don't mean to do it. But when we worry, we doubt God.

> "Jesus used this story to teach his followers that they should always pray and never lose hope."
>
> —Luke 18:1 NCV

3. How could we possibly think that an all-powerful God might lose his grip? Or that an all-knowing God might make a mistake? Scripture is very clear. God *is* in control.

Psalm 115:3: "Our God is in heaven. He **does** what he **pleases**" (NCV).

Isaiah 43:13: "I have **always** been God . . . . When I do something, no one can **change** it" (NCV).

Isaiah 46:10: "When I **plan** something, it **happens**. What I **want** to do, I **will** do" (NCV).

Lamentations 3:37: "Nobody can **speak** and have it happen **unless** the Lord **commands** it" (NCV).

Acts 2:23: "This was God's **plan** which he had made **long ago**; he knew all this would **happen**" (NCV).

Acts 17:25: "This God is the One who gives life, breath, and everything else to people. He does not need any **help** from them; he has **everything** he **needs**" (NCV).

Ephesians 1:11: "In Christ we were chosen to be God's people, because from the very beginning God had **decided** this in keeping with his **plan**. And he is the One who makes everything **agree** with what he **decides** and **wants**" (NCV).

According to the Bible, God is worthy of all the glory he receives. He does as he pleases. Who are we to question it? But we often have trouble accepting this truth because it goes against our own agenda. We pursue the wrong priorities. We want good friends, good talents, good money, and a good life. Our priority is *we*. God's priority, however, is God.

4. God always knows what's best. We don't always like it, but what else can we say?

○ What does Isaiah 45:7 say God is able to do?

"I made the light and the darkness. I bring peace, and I cause troubles. I, the Lord, do all these things" (Is. 45:7 NCV).

○ What does Solomon urge us to remember in Ecclesiastes 7:14?

"When life is good, enjoy it. But when life is hard, remember: God gives good times and hard times, and no one knows what tomorrow will bring" (Eccl. 7:14 NCV).

○ What does Lamentations 3:38 tell us God is able to command?

"Both bad and good things come by the command of the Most High God" (Lam. 3:38 NCV).

○ And according to Isaiah 48:10, 11, why does God do these things?

"I have made you pure, but not by fire, as silver is made pure. I have purified you by giving you troubles. I do this for myself, for my own sake. I will not let people speak evil against me, and I will not let some god take my glory" (Is. 48:10, 11 NCV).

> **"Don't look forward in fear, look backward in appreciation. God's proof is God's past. Forgetfulness sires fearfulness, but a good memory makes for a good heart."**
>
> **—Max Lucado**

Worry comes from the Greek word that means "to divide the mind." Anxiety splits us right down the middle, creating a double-minded thinker. Worry divides our perception. It distorts our vision. It saps our strength and wastes our energy. How on earth can we stop it? Paul offers a two-part answer: "Do not worry about anything, but pray and ask God for everything you need, always giving thanks" (Phil. 4:6 NCV). Our part in preventing worry includes prayer and gratitude.

5. The first strategy to purge the worry out of your life is prayer. Paul says not to worry, but to pray.

○ What does Luke 18:1 say we should always do, and never do?

<u>Jesus said that his followers should "always pray and never lose hope" (Luke 18:1 NCV).</u>

○ Who should pray, according to James 5:13?

<u>"Anyone who is having troubles should pray." (James 5:13 NCV).</u>

○ How does Paul say we should pray in Colossians 4:2?

<u>And Paul says that we should "continue praying" (Col. 4:2 NCV). Don't stop praying.</u>

6. The second thing Paul urges is thanksgiving. Worry has a hard time taking hold of a heart that's busy thanking God for his faithfulness in the past. Why should we be thankful, according to Psalm 107:8?

<u>"Oh, that men would give thanks to the LORD for His goodness, and for His wonderful works to the children of men!" (Ps. 107:8 NKJV).</u>

If our part is prayer and thanksgiving, what's God's part? Peace. Believing prayer ushers in God's peace. Not a random, spacey, earthly peace, but his peace. God doesn't battle anxiety. God enjoys perfect peace because God enjoys perfect power. And he offers his peace to you.

7. Peace

<u>b</u> Numbers 6:26   a. May the Lord of peace give you peace always.

<u>e</u> Luke 1:79   b. May the LORD watch over you and give you peace.

<u>c</u> John 14:27   c. Peace I leave with you; My peace I give to you.

<u>d</u> Romans 3:17   d. Only those who belong to God will find peace.

<u>a</u> 2 Thessalonians 3:16   e. God will guide our feet into the way of peace.

Peace is precious because there is no substitute. Lust may masquerade as love, and happiness might try to stand in for joy, but there is no mimic for peace. It's deep and it's real.

8. What is the peace of God able to do, according to Philippians 4:7?

   <u>"The peace of God, which surpasses all understanding, will guard your hearts and minds through Christ Jesus" (Phil. 4:7 NKJV). God's peace is an amazing thing. It does something that is beyond belief, something that defies comprehension. The peace of God is able to guard your mind. What's more, it is able to guard your heart. When the peace of God is in place, you cannot be defeated by life's worries and fears.</u>

9. If we want a heart filled with peace rather than worry, what must we let peace do, according to Colossians 3:15?

   <u>"Let the peace of God rule in your hearts, to which also you were called in one body; and be thankful" (Col. 3:15 NKJV). Let peace rule. Let it. Don't allow worries to drown out its quiet voice. Tune your ears to it. Hang on to its promise. And let it reign in your life.</u>

Letting go of worries means letting God know that you trust him. We need to let peace rule in our hearts. Sure, worries and fears might try to usurp the throne, but we don't have to let them. The peace that rules our hearts can also guard our hearts.

10. What does 1 Peter 5:7 say that we should do with all our worries and cares?

   "Casting all your care upon Him, for He cares for you"
   (1 Pet. 5:7 NKJV). Give them up. Pitch them aside. Cast
   them on to the One who is strong enough to bear
   them. But whatever you do, don't cling to them.

"Cast." Not place, lay, or occasionally offer. It's a strong verb. Peter enlists the same verb gospel writers used to describe the way Jesus treated demons. "He cast them out." An authoritative hand on the collar, another on the belt, and a "Don't come back." Here's something exciting: you can do the same with your fears! Get serious with them. Immediately cast them upon God. He's given you the authority—but you've got to claim it.

CONCLUSION

God can lead you into a worry-free world. Amazing, but true. So be quick to pray. Focus less on the problems ahead and more on the victories behind. Trust his sovereignty. Let him be the Lord. You do your part and God will do his. He will guard your heart with his peace . . . a peace that passes understanding.

this week's prayer requests

PRAYER OF THE THIRSTY

We come once again to the prayer of the thirsty.

Lord, I come thirsty. I come to drink, to receive. I receive Your work on the cross and in Your resurrection. My sins are pardoned and my death is defeated. I receive Your energy. Empowered by Your Holy Spirit, I can do all things through Christ who gives me strength. I receive Your lordship. I belong to You. Nothing comes to me that hasn't passed through You. And I receive Your love. Nothing can separate me from Your love.

MEMORY VERSE

*"Be anxious for nothing,
but in everything by prayer and
supplication, with thanksgiving,
let your requests be made known
to God; and the peace of God,
which surpasses all understanding,
will guard your hearts and
minds through Christ Jesus."*

—Philippians 4:6, 7 NKJV

Suggested Reading for this Week from
Come Thirsty by Max Lucado:

○ Chapter 10: "In God We (Nearly) Trust" We know that
God knows what's best. We know that we don't. We
also know that God cares, so we can trust him.

○ Chapter 11: "Worry? You Don't Have To" Worry
changes nothing, and only shows that we aren't trusting
God to do as he promised.

○ Chapter 12: "Angels Watching Over You" When you
accept God's lordship in your life, you can be assured
that many mighty angels will guard you in all your ways.

○ Chapter 13: "With God as Your Guardian" God guards
those who turn to him.

PLUNGE! LEADER'S GUIDE

WELL

RECEIVE HIS UNENDING, UNFAILING LOVE.

WEEK 5

Abiding in God's Love

"As the Father loved Me, I also have loved you; abide in My love."

—John 15:9 NKJV

OPENING ACTIVITIES

OPTION 1: AT THE POOL!

Have everyone partner up (partnering two guys or two girls). Everyone tries to swim in pairs—one person does the arm movements while the other person holds onto the partner and does the leg movements. This game is best tried in the shallow end!

Discussion Questions for Afterward:

1. With some things, having two people slows you down, but with other things having two people is a huge help. What are some things you like to do alone? with someone else?

2. If going through our lives is like swimming, God's love is like the water. It's all around us, even if we forget to think about it. What are some ways God's love surrounds you?

3. How is Jesus the perfect partner for your life?

OPTION 2: OUTDOORS

You'll Need:

Several pieces of rope

Have everyone stand beside a partner and tie each others' two inside legs together. Give everyone a chance to practice walking together—then choose a finish line and have a three-legged race!

Discussion Questions for Afterward:

1. Was it easy or difficult to walk with your partner? It takes time to develop a workable rhythm with someone else. If you and God were in a three-legged race together, would you be right in sync or kind of wobbly?

2. With some things, having two people slows you down, but with other things having two people is a huge help. What are some things you like to do alone? with someone else?

3. How is Jesus the perfect partner for your life?

OPTION 3: INDOORS

You'll Need:

A bag of heart-shaped candy
Paper
Crayons or markers

Have everyone draw creative symbols of love and share their meaning with the group. Give out heart-shaped candy as a reminder of how close we are to God's heart.

READING SCRIPTURE OUT LOUD TOGETHER

- **Romans 5:8:** "God demonstrates His own love toward us, in that while we were still sinners, Christ died for us" (NKJV).

- **1 John 3:1:** "Behold what manner of love the Father has bestowed on us, that we should be called children of God!" (NKJV).

- **1 John 4:7, 8:** "Beloved, let us love one another, for love is of God; and everyone who loves is born of God and knows God. He who does not love does not know God, for God is love" (NKJV).

- **Jeremiah 31:3:** "I have loved you with an everlasting love; therefore with lovingkindness I have drawn you" (NKJV).

- **1 John 4:19:** "We love Him because He first loved us" (NKJV).

- **Romans 8:38, 39:** "Yes, I am sure that neither death, nor life, nor angels, nor ruling spirits, nothing now, nothing in the future, no powers, nothing above us, nothing below us, nor anything else in the whole world will ever be able to separate us from the love of God that is in Christ Jesus our Lord" (NCV).

DISCUSSION QUESTIONS

- Please take a few moments to review the outline of the *Come Thirsty* lessons again with your group before moving forward with this week's lesson.

During this study, we'll be learning about four ways our thirst can be satisfied: God's work, God's energy, God's lordship, and God's love. They're easy to remember. Just think of the acrostic W-E-L-L.

Receive Christ's **W**ork on the cross.
　　The **E**nergy of his Spirit.
　　　　His **L**ordship over your life.
　　　　　　His unending, unfailing **L**ove.

Drink deeply and often. And out of you will flow rivers of living water.

○ God loves everyone he has created, but there is a difference between *being* loved and *accepting* that love. How does the human heart change when it understands the love of God and then returns it?

○ As humans, we often love others *because of* who they are or what they have done. We might have ulterior motives. Often, we have conditions: "I will love you if you will . . ." or "I will love you as long as you
. . ." or "I will love you until . . ." What do we look for in the people we choose to love? What conditions or expectations do we have?

○ God loves because he is love, and that love is unconditional. Nothing we do can change his love. What hope does this give to sinners—to all of us?

○ We are invited to abide in Christ's love. What is this compared to? *(To abide in Christ's love is to make his love our home. Settle in. Set up housekeeping. Make ourselves comfortable. When you abide somewhere, you live there. You grow familiar with the surroundings. Also, according to Jesus, the branch models his definition of "abiding." The branch must be connected to the vine in order to live, grow, and bear fruit.)*

○ Can we influence God? Can we make him do anything? Can we affect him or change him? Why do we try to earn our place in his heart?

○ Why does knowing that we are loved change us? How does knowing that we are loved strengthen us?

OPEN UP THE GROUP TO QUESTIONS

Do you have any questions that came up during the week while you were reading either the book or the daily devotional readings?

"God has poured out his love to fill our hearts. He gave us his love through the Holy Spirit, whom God has given to us."

—Romans 5:5 NCV

INTRODUCTION

Are you familiar with 1 Corinthians 13? It's often referred to as the "Love Chapter" because it highlights many qualities of pure, godly love. "Love is patient. Love is kind. Love is not boastful or rude." These are familiar and reassuring words. Often, we are invited to insert our own name into the wording of the chapter, personalizing it to challenge ourselves to live up to it. "Jenna is not easily provoked. Brad thinks no evil. Allyson bears all things." But have you ever considered that all of these great qualities also apply to God in his love for us?

When we say that God loves us, we can rest assured that God's love for us is patient. His love for us is kind. In his great love for us, he bears with us when we mess up and rejoices when we choose good things. *Love never fails, and neither does God.*

1. When you want to learn about love, you have to start at the source. John, Jesus's best friend, was known as "the beloved disciple." What does he say in 1 John 4:7, 8?

   "**Beloved**, let us **love** one another, for **love** is of God; and everyone who **loves** is born of God and knows God. He who does not **love** does not know God, for **God is love**" (1 John 4:7, 8 NKJV).

2. What does God's love for us look like?

   ○ How did God demonstrate his love for us, according to Romans 5:8?

"God demonstrates His own love toward us, in that while we were still sinners, Christ died for us" (Rom. 5:8 NKJV).

○ When we are saved, what does God do, according to Romans 5:5?

God loved us enough to die for us. "The love of God has been poured out in our hearts by the Holy Spirit who was given to us" (Rom. 5:5 NKJV).

○ Because of God's great love for us, what does he call us, according to 1 John 3:1?

God's love is poured over us. We are drenched in it. "Behold what manner of love the Father has bestowed on us, that we should be called children of God" (1 John 3:1 NKJV). God loves us so much that he's adopted us into his family. He calls us his own children.

> "[God] loves you because he is he. He loves you because he decides to. Self-generated, uncaused, and spontaneous; His constant-level love depends on his choice to give it."
>
> —Max Lucado

God pours out his love on his children. It's more than bucketfuls. It's more than pond-fuls. It's more than lake-fuls. It's more than ocean-fuls. We're drenched in it. Saturated by it. Soaked to the skin. But we can't be soaked to the *soul* unless we drink it in.

3. How does Jeremiah 31:3 characterize God's love for us?

"I have loved you with an everlasting love; therefore with lovingkindness I have drawn you" (Jer. 31:3 NKJV). The Message paraphrases this verse: "I've never quit loving you and never will. Expect love, love, and more love!"

PLUNGE! LEADER'S GUIDE

We already know that God is changeless. "I am the LORD, I do not change" (Mal. 3:6 NKJV). So it's not surprising to discover that God's love is also changeless. "I have loved you with an everlasting love" (Jer. 31:3 NKJV). Everlasting. Eternal. Never-ending. Always. Ceaseless. Unchangeable. Forever. Ever after.

4. In what way does God show his love in Zephaniah 3:17?

"The LORD your God in your midst, the Mighty One, will save; He will rejoice over you with gladness. He will quiet you with his love, He will rejoice over you with singing" (Zeph. 3:17 NKJV).

5. When you're out on the ocean, you're completely surrounded by water. When you're up in an airplane, there's nothing but clouds and sky. Astronauts who leave our atmosphere are surrounded by star-flecked space. What surrounds believers, according to Ephesians 3:17–19?

Paul prays that, "You, being rooted and grounded in love, may be able to comprehend with all the saints what is the width and length and depth and height—to know the love of Christ which passes knowledge" (Eph. 3:17–19 NKJV). God surrounds us with his love.

> "You don't influence God's love. You can't impact the tree-ness of a tree, the sky-ness of the sky, or the rock-ness of a rock. Nor can you affect the love of God."
>
> —Max Lucado

Over and around us, as far as the eye can see and beyond. God's love for us is so great, we can't even begin to comprehend its immensity. Or its intensity. Paul prays that believers might root themselves into it, drawing strength from it. He wants us to catch a glimpse of something too big to grasp. It is beyond measure. It is unsearchable in its magnitude. For the love of God is as big as God. After all, God is love.

6. The pages of Scripture are filled with love. The love of God. The love of Jesus. The love of believers. Here is just a sampling. Match up each truth with the Bible passage where it's located.

<u>e</u> Psalm 36:7

a. The God of love will be with you.

<u>h</u> John 13:34

b. God makes his home with those he loves.

<u>b</u> John 14:23

c. Speak the truth in love.

<u>i</u> 2 Corinthians 5:14

d. There is comfort in love.

<u>a</u> 2 Corinthians 13:11

e. God's lovingkindness is precious to his children.

<u>m</u> Ephesians 2:4

f. Keep yourselves in the love of God.

<u>g</u> Ephesians 3:19

g. The love of Christ passes all knowledge.

<u>c</u> Ephesians 4:15

h. Love one another as I have loved you.

<u>k</u> Ephesians 5:2

i. The love of Christ compels us.

<u>d</u> Philippians 2:1

j. God directs our hearts into his love.

<u>l</u> Colossians 2:2

k. Walk in love.

<u>j</u> 2 Thessalonians 3:5

l. Believers are knit together in love.

<u>f</u> Jude 1:21

m. God has loved us with a great love.

7. What does Jesus ask us to do in John 15:9, 10?

"As the **Father loved** Me, I also have **loved** you; **abide** in My **love**. If you **keep** My **commandments**, you will **abide** in My **love**, just as I have kept My Father's **commandments** and **abide** in His **love**" (NKJV)

To abide in Christ's love means making his love our home. Settling in. Setting up housekeeping. Making ourselves comfortable. When you abide somewhere, you live there. You grow familiar with the surroundings. Jesus abided in God's love. We are invited to abide in Christ's. By doing so, "in this world we are like him" (1 John 4:17 NCV).

"He knows you better than you know you and he has reached his verdict. He loves you still. No discovery will disillusion him, no rebellion will dissuade him. He loves you with an everlasting love."

—Max Lucado

8. What is Jesus' idea of abiding, according to John 15:4, 5?

"Remain in me, and I will remain in you. A branch cannot produce fruit alone but must remain in the vine. In the same way, you cannot produce fruit alone but must remain in me. I am the vine, and you are the branches. If any remain in me and I remain in them, they produce much fruit. But without me they can do nothing" (John 15:4, 5 NCV).

Jesus uses the image of a branch as a model for his definition of "abiding." The branch has to stay connected to the vine in order to live, grow, and bear fruit. Without the vine, a branch is useless. It can't do anything. We need to hang on to Christ like a branch clutches the vine. If we don't, we get thirsty.

9. With a God who draws us with lovingkindness and promises everlasting love, how can we resist? What does 1 John 4:19 tell us is the response of believers to God's outpouring?

   "We love Him because He first loved us" (1 John 4:19 NKJV).

We can't earn God's love. We can't barter for it. We can't plead with God to love us, nor do we need to! It would be useless to try, because he already does. He loved us first. All we can do is respond to God's love, abide in his love, love him and other people in return.

10. What question does Paul raise in Romans 8:35? And what resounding promise is the answer, found in verses 38 and 39?

   Paul's question: "Can anything separate us from the love Christ has for us? Can troubles or problems or sufferings or hunger or nakedness or danger or violent death?" (Rom. 8:35 NCV). The answer: "Yes, I am sure that neither death, nor life, nor angels, nor ruling spirits, nothing now, nothing in the future, no powers, nothing above us, nothing below us, nor anything else in the whole world will ever be able to separate us from the love of God that is in Christ Jesus our Lord" (Rom. 8:38, 39 NCV).

Nothing can separate us from the love of God. Paul is totally convinced of this! "I am convinced that nothing can ever separate us from his love." In the original Greek, he uses the perfect tense, meaning—"I have become and I remain convinced." This is no passing idea or fluffy thought. It's a deeply rooted conviction. Paul is absolutely sure. You can be, too!

CONCLUSION

Nothing can shake your heavenly Father's love for you. God knows your entire story, from your first word to your final breath. And he declares, "You are mine." Run to the well of his love and drink to your heart's content. Not just occasional sips, but long swallows. Take your fill. The supply is boundless, everlasting. God's water fountain never runs dry.

this week's prayer requests

PRAYER OF THE THIRSTY

We return to this prayer of the thirsty soul. It's the prayer of a heart ready to receive God's love. Unconditional, unreserved, immeasurable love. Take the time each day to pray this prayer aloud. Let it remind your heart and mind just how precious you are to the Father.

Lord, I come thirsty. I come to drink, to receive. I receive Your work on the cross and in Your resurrection. My sins are pardoned and my death is defeated. I receive Your energy. Empowered by Your Holy Spirit, I can do all things through Christ who gives me strength. I receive Your lordship. I belong to You. Nothing comes to me that hasn't passed through You. And I receive Your love. Nothing can separate me from Your love.

MEMORY VERSE

"Yes, I am sure that neither death, nor life, nor angels, nor ruling spirits, nothing now, nothing in the future, no powers, nothing above us, nothing below us, nor anything else in the whole world will ever be able to separate us from the love of God that is in Christ Jesus our Lord."

—Romans 8:38, 39 NCV

Suggested Reading for this Week from
Come Thirsty by Max Lucado:

○ Chapter 14: "Going Deep" Plunge into the depths of the limitless love of God.

○ Chapter 15: "Have You Heard the Clanging Door?" Some fear they've gone too far, done too much, wandered too long to be worthy of God's love. But the God who knows everything about you loves you still.

○ Chapter 16: "Fearlessly Facing Eternity" God knows our imperfections, yet has chosen us. We need never fear God's judgment. Trust his love.

○ Chapter 17: "If God Wrote You a Letter" If God sent you a personal letter, it might read something like this.

RECEIVE CHRIST'S WORK ON THE CROSS.

RECEIVE THE ENERGY OF HIS SPIRIT.

RECEIVE HIS LORDSHIP OVER YOUR LIFE.

RECEIVE HIS UNENDING, UNFAILING LOVE.

WELL

WEEK 6

If God Wrote You a Letter

"The LORD will guide you continually, and satisfy your soul in drought, and strengthen your bones; you shall be like a watered garden, and like a spring of water, whose waters do not fail."

—Isaiah 58:11 NKJV

FOR THE LEADER

OPENING ACTIVITIES

OPTION 1: AT THE POOL!

Choose one person to be "It." That person gets out of the pool and faces away from it while everyone else is gathered in the water behind him/her. The "It" person calls out a category (e.g. "Olympic swimmers"), and the other players think of a word/name in that category. (Categories can be anything from colors to ice cream flavors, but encourage everyone to try to choose a category that relates to water. Examples might include types of drinks, places to swim, famous swimmers, etc.). Each person whispers his/her word to someone else to make sure no one forgets or changes. "It" starts calling out words in the category. When players' words are called, they try to swim across the pool quietly without being heard. If the "It" person hears a player moving, he/she can jump in and try to tag the person before s/he reaches the other side. If a player gets tagged, s/he becomes "It"—otherwise, the last person whose word hasn't been called becomes the next "It."

Discussion Questions for Afterward:

1. What are some things you've learned these past few weeks about spiritual thirst and God's living water?

2. In this game, whoever is "It" spends a lot of time listening. Do you ever feel like you're trying to listen for God to speak, but you can't hear a thing? How does it feel? What do you do?

3. What is your favorite water image from *Come Thirsty* or *Plunge!?* What does it reveal about God?

OPTION 2: OUTDOORS

You'll Need:

Several water balloons

Have an old-fashioned water balloon toss. Everyone stands across from a partner. After a few practice tosses, each person begins taking a step back every time she catches the water balloon. As players toss the balloon, have them shout out something they've learned about during this study.

Discussion Questions for Afterward:

1. What lessons did you call out that you've learned these past few weeks?

2. Sometimes relationships are described as tossing a ball back and forth. What are some ways that God "tosses the ball" to us? In what ways do we toss it back? Relate an instance when you know you dropped the ball.

3. What is your favorite water image from *Come Thirsty* or *Plunge!?* What does it reveal about God?

OPTION 3: INDOORS

You'll Need:

Paper & pencils

Arrange groups of four. Tell each group, "Pretend you're going to write a letter from God to your church. What will it say?" Spend some time thinking and writing (remember to be respectful!). Then, come back together and read the letters aloud.

READING SCRIPTURE OUT LOUD TOGETHER

○ **Isaiah 55:1:** "Ho! Everyone who thirsts, come to the waters" (NKJV).

○ **Colossians 2:10:** "You are complete in Him, who is the head of all principality and power." (NKJV).

○ **Isaiah 38:17:** "You have lovingly delivered my soul from the pit of corruption, for You have cast all my sins behind Your back" (NKJV).

○ **2 Corinthians 4:1:** "As we have received mercy, we do not lose heart" (NKJV)

○ **Romans 8:32:** "He who did not spare His own Son, but delivered Him up for us all, how shall He not with Him also freely give us all things?" (NKJV).

○ **Isaiah 26:3:** "You will keep him in perfect peace, whose mind is stayed on You, because he trusts in You" (NKJV).

○ **Psalm 139:10:** "Even there Your hand shall lead me, and Your right hand shall hold me" (NKJV).

DISCUSSION QUESTIONS

○ Take a few minutes to review the lessons of the last several weeks. The outline is simple, but the concepts themselves are rich and complex.

During this study, we'll be learning about four ways our thirst can be satisfied: God's work, God's energy, God's lordship, and God's love. They're easy to remember. Just think of the acrostic W-E-L-L.

Receive Christ's **W**ork on the cross.
The **E**nergy of his Spirit.
His **L**ordship over your life.
His unending, unfailing **L**ove.

Drink deeply and often. And out of you will flow rivers of living water.

○ Scripture is filled with promises. This week's "Letter from God" holds many of these precious promises. What makes these promises more trustworthy than the promises of people?

○ If the promises of God are so certain, do you really believe them? If you believe them, do you act upon them?

○ Now that you know about the W-E-L-L and have spent the last few weeks drinking from it, are you finished? Can you move on now? What do you think about returning to these things continually?

○ Work. Energy. Lordship. Love. Which of these four has come into clearer focus for you over the last five weeks? What lessons have you learned?

OPEN UP THE GROUP TO QUESTIONS

Do you have any questions that came up during the week while you were reading either the book or the daily devotional readings?

INTRODUCTION

The final chapter of Max Lucado's book *Come Thirsty* asks you to pause and consider, what if God wrote you a letter? In a way, he did. What we have come to call the Bible is a long love letter from the Father's heart to his people. Max takes the time to condense God's message in a way that speaks to our thirsting hearts. Let's take a more careful look at the promises this letter holds.

We'll take the letter in small sections. Take your time. Meditate over each of these verses. Let them sink in. Think about what God is telling you about himself. What does he want you to know? What is he promising you? Then give yourself time to respond. What would happen if this was a two-way conversation? What would be your reply? Consider what you would like to tell God in return.

IF GOD WROTE YOU A LETTER

Are you thirsty? Come and drink. I am the One who comforts you. I bought you. I complete you. I delight in you and claim you as my own, rejoicing over you as a bridegroom rejoices over his bride. I will never fail nor forsake you.

<u>e</u> Isaiah 55:1

<u>c</u> Isaiah 51:12

<u>a</u> 1 Corinthians 6:20

<u>f</u> Colossians 2:10

<u>b</u> Isaiah 62:4, 5

<u>d</u> Hebrews 13:5

a. You were bought at a price.

b. The LORD delights in you and rejoices over you.

c. I am He who comforts you.

d. He will never leave you nor forsake you.

e. Everyone who thirsts, come to the waters.

f. You are complete in Him.

ACCEPT MY WORK

I know your many mistakes and your mighty sins, yet my grace is sufficient for you. I have cast all your sins behind my back, trampled them under my feet, and thrown them into the depths of the ocean! Your sins have been washed away, swept away like the morning mists, scattered like the clouds. O return to me, for I have paid the price to set you free.

d Amos 5:12

a. God has cast all your sins behind His back.

f 2 Corinthians 12:9

b. You have been washed, sanctified, justified.

a Isaiah 38:17

c. Our transgressions have been blotted out.

e Micah 7:19

d. He knows all about your transgressions.

b 1 Corinthians 6:11

e. All our sins have been cast into the sea.

c Isaiah 44:22

f. God's grace is sufficient.

Your death is swallowed up in victory. I disarmed the evil rulers and authorities and broke the power of the devil, who had the power of death. Blessed are those who die in the Lord. Your citizenship is in heaven. Come, inherit the kingdom prepared for you where I will remove all of your sorrows, and there will be no more death or sorrow or crying or pain.

e 1 Corinthians 15:54

a. Blessed are those who die in the Lord.

b Colossians 2:15

b. Principalities and powers have been disarmed.

_f_ Hebrews 2:14

   c. We shall inherit a kingdom prepared for us.

_a_ Revelation 14:13

   d. Every tear shall be wiped away.

_g_ Philippians 3:20

   e. Death is swallowed up in victory.

_d_ Matthew 25:34

   f. He has destroyed the devil's power over death.

_c_ Revelation 21:4

   g. Our citizenship is in heaven.

RELY ON MY ENERGY

You are worried and troubled about many things; trust me with all your heart. I know how to rescue godly people from their trials. My Spirit helps you in your distress. Let me strengthen you with my glorious power. I did not spare my Son but gave him up for you. Won't I give you everything else? March on, precious soul, with courage! Never give up. I will help you. I will uphold you.

_e_ Luke 10:41

   a. We are strengthened by God's glorious power.

_i_ Proverbs 3:5

   b. We do not lose heart.

_d_ 2 Peter 2:9

   c. God gives us freely of all the things we need.

_g_ Romans 8:26

   d. The Lord knows how to deliver the godly.

_a_ Colossians 1:11

   e. You are worried and troubled about many things.

_c_ Romans 8:32

   f. March on in strength.

_f_ Judges 5:21

   g. The Spirit helps us in our weaknesses.

_b_ 2 Corinthians 4:1   h. God will help you. He will uphold you.

_h_ Isaiah 41:10   i. Trust in the LORD with all your heart.

TRUST MY LORDSHIP

Trust in me always. I am the eternal Rock, your Shepherd, the Guardian of your soul. When you go through deep waters and great trouble, I will be with you. When you go through rivers of difficulty, you will not drown! When you walk through the fire of oppression, you will not be burned up; the flames will not consume you.

_b_ Isaiah 26:3, 4   a. He is the Shepherd and Overseer of our souls.

_a_ 1 Peter 2:25   b. God will keep us in perfect peace.

_c_ Isaiah 43:2   c. He will be with you through everything.

So don't worry. I never tire nor sleep. I stand beside you. My angels have set up camp around you. I hide you in the shelter of my presence. I will go ahead of you directing your steps and delighting in every detail of your life. If you stumble, you will not fall, for I hold you by the hand. I will guide you along the best pathway for your life. Wars will break out near and far, but don't panic. I have overcome the world. Don't worry about anything; instead, pray about everything. I surround you with a shield of love.

i Matthew 6:34 a. Be strong, don't be afraid, God goes with you.

c Psalm 121:3 b. He holds our hand and leads us.

f Psalm 34:7 c. He who keeps you will not slumber.

j Psalm 31:20 d. He has overcome the world.

a Deuteronomy 31:6 e. Don't fear when you hear rumors of war.

h Psalm 37:23, 24 f. The angel of the LORD encamps around God's people.

b Psalm 139:10 g. The LORD will bless the righteous.

e Matthew 24:6 h. The LORD orders our steps and upholds us.

d John 16:33 i. Do not worry about tomorrow.

k Philippians 4:6 j. God will hide us and keep us secretly.

g Psalm 5:12 k. Be anxious for nothing, but pray.

I will make you fruitful in the land of suffering, trading beauty for ashes, joy for mourning, praise for despair. I live with the worried, the sad, the stressed, the crushed. I put a new spirit in you and get you on your feet again. I give you reason to live. Weeping may go on all night, but joy comes with the morning. If I am for you, who can ever be against you?

c Genesis 41:52 a. God dwells with those who are humble.

e Isaiah 61:1–3 b. Joy comes in the morning.

<u>a</u> Isaiah 57:15   c. God has caused me to be fruitful.

<u>b</u> Psalm 30:5   d. If God is for us, who can be against us?

<u>d</u> Romans 8:31   e. God will trade beauty for your ashes.

RECEIVE MY LOVE

I throw my arms around you, lavish attention on you and guard you like the apple of my eye. I rejoice over you with great gladness. My thoughts of you cannot be counted; they outnumber the grains of sand! Nothing can ever separate you from my love. Death can't, and life can't. The angels can't, and the demons can't. Your fears for today, your worries about tomorrow, and even the powers of hell can't keep my love away.

<u>d</u> Deuteronomy 32:10   a. Nothing can separate us from Christ's love.

<u>b</u> Zephaniah 3:17   b. God will save you, rejoice over you, quiet you.

<u>c</u> Psalm 139:17, 18   c. God's thoughts of you are precious.

<u>a</u> Romans 8:35   d. We are kept as the apple of God's eye.

You sometimes say, "The Lord has deserted us; the Lord has forgotten us." But can a mother forget her nursing child? Can she feel no love for a child she has borne? But even if that were possible, I would not forget you! I paid for you with the precious lifeblood of Christ, my sinless, spotless Lamb. No one will snatch you away from me. See, I have written your name on my hand. I call you my friend. Why, the very hairs on your head are all numbered. So don't be afraid; you are incredibly valuable to me.

_e_ Isaiah 49:14, 15   a. No one can snatch us from His hand.

_b_ 1 Peter 1:19   b. You're bought with Christ's precious blood.

_a_ John 10:28   c. Even your hairs are numbered.

_f_ Isaiah 49:16   d. Christ has called you His friends.

_d_ John 15:15   e. God cannot forget you.

_c_ Matthew 10:29–31   f. Your name is inscribed on His hands.

Give me your burdens; I will take care of you. I know how weak you are, that you are made of dust. Give all your worries and problems to me, for I care about what happens to you. Remember, I am right here. Come to me when you are tired and carry heavy burdens, and I will give you rest. I delight in you: and I can be trusted to keep my promise. Come and drink the water of life.

_d_ Psalm 55:22   a. The Lord is at hand.

_g_ Psalm 103:13, 14   b. If you thirst, come and drink freely.

_e_ 1 Peter 5:7   c. The LORD takes pleasure in His people

_a_ Philippians 4:5   d. Cast your burden on the LORD; He will sustain you.

<u>h</u> Matthew 11:28

<u>c</u> Psalm 149:4

<u>f</u> Hebrews 10:23

<u>b</u> Revelation 22:17

e. Cast your cares upon Him, He cares for you.

f. He who makes us promises is faithful.

g. God remembers that we are made of dust.

h. Come to Me and I will give you rest.

Your Maker, Your Father,
With all My love,
God

CONCLUSION

Promises. Each and every one of those verses you just looked up holds precious and powerful promises. Do you believe them? Then soak in them. Drink them up. And don't stop there. Drink, and keep drinking. Return to them, and to the One who promised them. He holds everything you will ever need.

PRAYER OF THE THIRSTY

One more time, pray the prayer of the thirsty. But don't let it be the last time. You can't saturate a dehydrated heart with one quick gulp. Return over and over to let God's promises soak in. Let this prayer remind you of the wellspring of life—God's work, his energy, his lordship, and his love. It's all yours: all you have to do is ask.

> Lord, I come thirsty. I come to drink, to receive. I receive Your work on the cross and in Your resurrection. My sins are pardoned and my death is defeated. I receive Your energy. Empowered by Your Holy Spirit, I can do all things through Christ who gives me strength. I receive Your lordship. I belong to You. Nothing comes to me that hasn't passed through You. And I receive Your love. Nothing can separate me from Your love.

MEMORY VERSE

"The LORD will guide you continually, and satisfy your soul in drought, and strengthen your bones; you shall be like a watered garden, and like a spring of water, whose waters do not fail."

—Isaiah 58:11 NKJV

this week's prayer requests

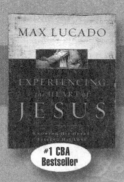
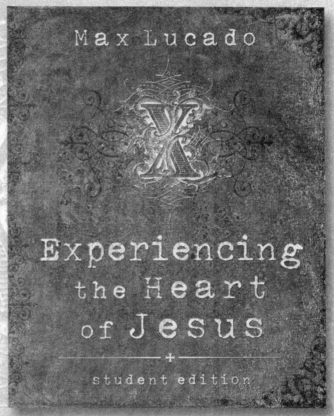